FRANCES THOMAS was born in Wales, where she now lives, having spent many years in London. She has written various books for adults and children, including a biography of Christina Rossetti. She has won the Welsh Arts Council's Tir na nOg prize four times for her children's books. She has also written two 'poetry journals', *A Bracelet of Bright Hair* and *Dancing in the Chequered Shade*. Her most recent work is the *Girls of Troy* quartet, published by SilverWood Books. For more information, visit her website at www.francesthomas.org.

Also By Frances Thomas

Helen's Daughter

The Burning Towers

The Silver-Handled Knife

The Beautiful One

The Memory Gate

Poems by
Frances Thomas

SilverWood

Independently published in 2020
This edition published by SilverWood Books in 2020

SilverWood Books Ltd
14 Small Street, Bristol, BS1 1DE, United Kingdom
www.silverwoodbooks.co.uk

ISBN 978-1-80042-042-7 (paperback)

Page design and typesetting by SilverWood Books

The Memory Gate

To my family: Richard, Harriet, Lucy, Matthew, Lily and Jacob –
for the best of memories.

Contents

THE MEMORY GATE

ᥴᥱ

The Memory Gate

A road winds upward. A castle somewhere,

Or is it a church? Old houses. Shops. *Tabac…*

Oh, are we in France? But how did we get here?

Where were we going, and why?

The gate shuts fast.

It's dark, and often locked. Sometimes it lets you in,

Spits out fragments, bits and pieces.

There's seventy-six years of stuff in there, after all,

Crammed like an old tramp's shopping cart.

That hill, that town, a dozen others like it. That face (it's not
      good at faces).

The picture trembles for a moment on the brink of focus,

Then it's gone.

Why did we quarrel? What was her name?

Who was in that film? That book? Name beginning with 'P'?

Or 'J', maybe…

The gate shuts fast again.

Cathedral

Bishops lie with smashed faces,

A nice lady shows us to our seats.

There is a tea-urn behind the high altar

And a corner with cushions and toys for the children.

All colour has gone from the walls,

The great pillars are elephant grey

And only the jewelled windows shine out.

There are hand-made kneelers in our pews,

But nobody kneels now.

Instead we sit, bemused, wondering whether this is chancel or
   apse.

Peasants used to stand here trembling;

Their God would send them to hell soon as look at them.

God has got kinder now,

But we don't quite see the point of it all,

We know it's beautiful and must be cherished,

And we like the way the town stops and turns medieval around it.

We like the shining glass and mourn the empty niches of the
   saints.

We have coffee and buy a postcard for a friend:

Here for a week. Hotel okay. Cathedral beautiful.

And then we sit and wonder what to do next.

But nobody kneels…

Wallbrook

The Romans would have liked all this,

This glass, this marble,

These cathedrals of wealth and splendour.

When they tramped the clay in their studded boots,

The little river still ran through cress and kingcups,

And birds sang out in scrubby trees.

It was a good place to build a temple;

To last, they thought, for ever, like themselves.

Now we go down, down

To where a divine boy in a Phrygian cap is killing a bull.

He does not mind us,

He's been alone for two thousand years

Intent only on his sacrifice,

Unworshipped, unadorned.

Back into the light, we see the spired church of a different god.

The river's curve still shapes the road,

Though now it is buried deep with lost coins, broken knives.

Does it rage down there or trickle gently?

Does it miss sunshine and sky?

Nobody knows, nobody sees it, hears it now.

But London's gone quiet here in this little street; holds its breath.

While traffic roars beyond, and wind blows dust,

The Romans and the river

Long gone, long forgotten.

Sutton Hoo

Once all this was his, the shining river,
The wind-scoured sky, the black pines.
Smoke from his mead-hall rose strong and straight,
Warriors and shield-wall guarded his bounds.
When he died, they hauled his great ship up the hill
And crammed it full of treasures.
But then, all was forgotten, even his name.
Till one day, Mrs Pretty saw warriors in her misty field
And sent for nice Mr Brown who understood these things.
They dug deep, deep into the hill, but found no king, no ship.
But the treasures glittered still, the gold, the garnets, the great
    helm.
Now people search these spaces for the king who isn't there,
Trying to tell his story, with only his gold
And a ghost ship to help them. Archaeologists expect such
    endings.

But then, perhaps, all was as he meant, and in a winter darkness,
Sky glittering with stars,
The great ship broke free from its mound, scattering soil as it rose,
And flew on night-wings across Suffolk skies,

To the distant north and a warrior heaven

Where he was greeted with loud praise-song

And a shield-wall finer

Than his own had ever been.

Brancusi

I think of the seashore. The light rising
Cold, bone-bleached, the white sky.
Now stone puffs and pouts into breath
Polished like a shell, plump as eggs.
A feather-furl of gold, a grey wing.
Sea sings through stone hollows,
The air is clean as a bell;
Wood, stone and beaten gold
Inhabit their spaces
With cool certainty.
I think of the seashore. There are no walls.

Daphne

I never wanted this,
My straight white legs sucked
Into mud, grasping at nothing,
My veins dry,
The pump of my heart stilled.
My mouth makes a red hole;
No sound comes out.

What price my virtue now,
Turned all to leaf and branch.
He should have been transformed, not I.
But he was a god, and I was
Expendable.

I am of the forest now.
Trees, uncaring, stare at me.
I am not one of them,
Will never be.
I will die in another way.
But they are my family now.

Exiles

He sent us out naked
So we didn't know how cold the nights would be,
But how bright the stars would blaze
In that place, flowers never died,
And the green leaves shone like wax;
It became boring.
He was our friend,
Till we asked questions.
He didn't like that.
The angels wept –
They were sorry to see us go.
They said the world was hateful,
But we loved it, the wilderness,
The charging streams, the blue hills.
And though He cursed me with pain,
I had children, many children –
I spread them across the world.
My blood pumps through you all.
And he, my tall, strong man
Learned to bend Nature to his will,
To dig, to plough, to plant, to harvest.

All that he touched grew strong.

All because we once asked why…

Gemini

Beautiful boys,
Love bound you
Tight as buds on a stem.
Death only sent you spinning
Into a cold sky.

On earth you shone,
One mortal, one divine –
No one could tell,
You shone the same.

Death took you by surprise,
You shouldn't have died;
The gods wept.
Only the sky would do.

Beautiful boys,
Love could not save you,
But holds you now,
Still bright in the blackness.

Orchid

It came out of darkness,
Windless, soilless, scentless,
Caressed by no bee, brushed by no rain,
A Hades-flower, white-petalled and heavy,
Arched stems and grasping roots.

He made it to please her, because he loved her,
Lonely Persephone, who thirsted for cool breezes,
And the brush of grass against her feet.
Did she weep in the darkness when he gave it to her,
Remembering thyme-scented hills and the scud of clouds?
Or did she smile at it, and learn to love
A different kind of beauty?

A Song for Fanny Imlay

Invisible girl,
Who thinks of you now?
Who cared for you then?

Not your smart sisters.
They got their poets;
You got no-one.
Your mother cared, probably,
But then she died:
You were three years old,
There was no-one to love you.

In that dark house
Talk was the currency;
How they all talked!
Coleridge came and he went,
Shelley came and stayed.
You might have loved him,
But he didn't see you.

He you named *Papa*

Called you 'not unprepossessing.'
Mary, the clever one,
Claire, the bold,
Had their adventures,
You stayed in the dark house,
Related to no-one.
You had nowhere to go,

It was your prison:
While your sisters shared poets
Under Italian skies.

You went a long way to die,
You didn't mean to be found;
Died quietly, making no fuss.
You must have wept,
But there was no one to hear.
Wrote that your birth
'Was unfortunate,'
And your life
Just 'a series of pain.'
You were just twenty-two.
No-one went to your funeral,
They left no memorial,

Made no picture.

Your grave is unknown.

Invisible girl,

We hold the door open for you,

But you still don't come out;

You never learned the knack.

Fanny Imlay was the illegitimate daughter of Mary Wollstonecraft, step-daughter to William Godwin and half-sister to Mary (later Shelley). Claire Clairmont was a stepsister by Godwin's second marriage. Fanny committed suicide aged twenty-two.

Marmalade

She made marmalade; it was good marmalade;
She did everything well.
I had it on my shelf for ages,
And then didn't eat it because she was dead.

The loved dead gather around in the shadows,
Too many of them now.
They whisper *Remember us! Remember us!*
Read our books, tell our jokes,
Talk about that day in the garden,
Just remember who we were.
We don't want to be forgotten...

But I didn't eat her marmalade;
It seemed disrespectful.
So it sat there, amber and glowing in its jar.
A year went by; another.
The marmalade lasted longer than she had done.
People don't last, that's the point.
We don't forget them, though we're unsure how to remember.
We talk to them, but they don't talk back.

We make up words for them; *'what he would have wanted...*
Didn't she always like...?'
But their likings are nowhere now.
In the end, I put the marmalade on my breakfast toast;
It's all gone now.

Dear Emily...

Dear Emily,

Forgive me for disturbing your...peace, I would say,

But I don't suppose peace is really what you want.

You get on quite well with God, I should think,

Striding the heavenly hills, looking ahead, and never behind,
    nor around.

I know what I say won't please you,

(Though your sister agreed with me; she thought you'd made
    a monster.)

Think of all those teenage girls, whose lives you ruined,

Making us believe we wanted *him*, dark, brooding, full of anguish.

We thought – fat chance – we could save him.

He would become our lover for all our days, this cross dark man.

He strangled puppies – how come we didn't notice *that*?

Let him grapple his own demons,

And give us back our girlhood years.

Give us a man who smiles and strokes kittens,

Someone we can live with, without torment.

Let him go his own mad, lonely way.

Let's face it, he was an *arsehole,* Emily.

The Name That Nobody Knows

Somewhere you have a name that nobody knows,

Not even you,

Your secret name,

Though at night you might dream it

You'll unremember it by morning,

Or it might slip from your unconscious doodling hands,

Onto crumpled paper,

It won't be there when you call for it.

But you'll hear it one day,

Coming from a treeline of shadows

At twilight when the colours go,

Or when the light falls in strands over the hill,

Just as you close your eyes,

You'll hear your secret name,

You'll try to say 'I'm coming,'

But the words don't come

And your eyes fall shut

On your name forever.

The Dark Square

The dark square over my head
Will be the last darkness I see.
I have watched all night;
No stars, no moon, look back at me –
The darkness is complete.
My women snore gently;
If I woke them, they'd watch with me,
But they'd lament – what use is that?

Instead, I think of what can be no more;
The French court, all silks and sibilance;
Ah, I should have married a French prince.

The King, the King! they call,
And in he stumps, his small eyes peering,
His fat hands, his little prick.
I never loved him really,
Though he loved me to distraction – once –
See, his letters prove it;
Mine own sweetheart…would you were in mine arms…

I had jewels, cloth-of-gold. When I spoke, all listened.
When I laughed they laughed with me.
I drank power like wine;
But all was *his* in the end.

The fat Spaniard died of grief,
Gracious to the end, they said.
(The people always liked her best.)
How I despised her, and those dead babies.
But we are the same now,
Cast into his darkness.

And for him, the little mouse girl,
Mouse-eyes and twitching nose.
He'll kill her too in the end, one way or another.

How will my child fare? My little red-haired one –
Alone in a world of enemies? Will she be strong?
Will she meet her mother's fate?
I hate to leave her – but I have no choice.
They say it's quick – and my neck is small.

A woman moans and mutters in her sleep;

Doors clang, footsteps echo.

The dark square pales – I must go and die.

The Beloved

O poet lurching hugely through your landscape
crying your love,
so that stones bleed and the white moon weeps,
what a giant you are
and how still the small voice of your beloved
as she sits in the dust
hair sifting gold on her skin.

Yet your love scorns
her because
her voice runs dry to your waterfall,
your rushing floods:

how can she escape,
her small self netted in your poetry,

and how she must hate you
now you have fixed her
silent as marble
and as barren as gold.

Song of the Bookish Girl

Oh how I hated netball! The smelly changing rooms,

Chapped thighs in baggy sexless shorts;

Those great hulking jumping girls,

Aertex shirts stained at the armpits;

And me, searching for the spot of least action,

Hoping not to be seen from the road.

And then some days, the teacher despairing said,

You're useless, Thomas.

Go and sit in the library till the bell.

The library! Yess!

The Memory of Houses

Look now at this house, brass knocker, trees in tubs.

She hangs curtains, strips floors, paints Farrow and Ball…

But the house knows better; by that fireplace (original feature)

Old Jack puffed at his pipe and spat out phlegm,

Was to die in what's now called 'The Master,' coughing still.

Maggie gave birth there five times;

One died, and his pale body was laid out there too.

The other four shuddered at the corpse which they were forced
    to kiss,

But then ran out to play in the street,

Scrumped apples from the corner house,

Pulled down Mrs Green's washing and ran off laughing.

They said, later, those days were 'paradise'

Though poor Maggie didn't think so, her husband dead

And her hands red with toil.

Chambermaid Lizzy knew every inch of those stairs, (a 'fine curved
    balustrade.')

Trudging up with buckets, and down with chamber-pots.

Her Mister owned a pharmacy. A real fusspot, she said,

But what can you do? You have to work.

Ernest and May, who hadn't built a shelter

Sat rigid with fear, while bombs fell all around.

One got number 43, killed the old girl and her cat.

But they lived on, to see their children settled nicely:

Barbara was a teacher, while Ronnie worked in a bank,

And Jill married a man who owned two garages

But the next lot threw all their stuff out and put in a proper
kitchen.

The house watched it going in;

And coming out again, when the next ones came.

They said 'they'd never leave'; put in everything new

And a magazine came and took pictures.

Their children never played in the street, of course.

But the house was too small when the new baby came.

(Maggie's lot had slept two to a bed, all in the one room;

Though this wouldn't do for them. The house knew that.)

A young couple, city-workers, who thought a million small
change.

Wouldn't stay long, had itchy feet. The house would watch
them come,

Will watch them go; all those memories rushing by,

All those lives passing briefly through,

Thinking they belonged; and now they're gone.

That's how it is with houses,
Their memories are longer than ours
And they know much more.

Kiss

I didn't kiss properly, my uncle said.
I had to learn to kiss.
And he of course would show me how…
The family were all watching.
We never kissed much at home.
Or hugged, or whispered 'Love you, bye…'
People didn't then.

Though aunties proffered powdered cheeks,
And those fur tippets' eyes, which stared at you.
But *properly?* Something wrong was here,
Would rather not, but had no choice.
You did what you were told.

So I, my uncle said, didn't do it right.
I had to learn to do it (I was ten).
Something about *being a proper woman…*
I squeezed my eyes shut.
He went and showed me how.
I remember just that bristly wetness,
And how he held it there a tad too long.

The watching family never said a word.

Well, people didn't then.

Journey

My father expected a taxi.
'The worst thing is the waiting,' he said.

The sun always deceives
Shining through dirty glass,
Seagulls crying on the rubbish heaps.
But the road curves back into darkness,
The driver is dumb,
And you don't get your money back.
We don't talk about it really,
Believe that the sun will save us,
Just so long as it shines.

My father's taxi never came.
He went anyway.

Sparrowhawk

You can't believe the speed.
The cycling mugger I saw
The other day on Southgate Road
Would have been proud

Of such a swoop,
Focussed, pure energy,
The gilt glint of claws,
The steel eye,
The fall of tiny feathers.

The small birds scatter
In a cloud of fear;
The trees fall silent.

Laugharne, September

The tide is out,
And there is just this bay,
A stretch of bright sandbanks and small pools
Through which black birds trip daintily,
Ankle-deep in silver, leaving tiny tracks.

The sky is a colour you can't describe,
Not white, not blue, not platinum,
Neither paint nor camera will render
Its pure clarity, like an angel's wings,
Or the sheen of an old photograph.
The eye is the only pure receptor,
And that eye will be somewhere else tomorrow,
Seeing supermarkets, petrol stations, privet hedges.
All that gleaming light just a memory.
It is yours, though now,
Yours and yours alone, to hoard through winter
(For days like this will seldom come).

Llanleonfell Church

They don't mean you to find it,

This church planted high among trees,

In wintery colours of bronze and rust.

No sign, and the road just a rough and potholed track.

A farm notice snarls *BEWARE OF DOGS.*

But I find a Christmas rose on the dead oak leaves,

Its white petals curled like a baby's fist

And inside the gate, the graves are clean and set with flowers.

The church is clean, too, clean and well-kept,

Flowers, candles, banners and cloths;

A weathered Roman gravestone;

They were here too, it seems.

And a Wesley got married here

In this quietest of quiet places,

He and his bride and all their kin,

Trudging across fields in their wedding clothes;

Would have arrived with muddy hems,

But it was the place they wanted to be.

People still come here, secretly it seems,

Leave flowers at gravesides and candles in their stands.

It is still the place they want to be.

The Last Wolf

When the last wolf died
And its paws nailed to the church door,
The black hills wept,
Nights fell silent,
The moon was swallowed in clouds,
Trees huddled together.
Only rats' claws now
Score tracks in the mud;
The glinting eyes, the huge paws,
The howls stretched out in sad music,
Gone, gone forever.

Shepherds rejoiced for a while,
But they were sad too;
Even a bitter enemy can be missed,
And mourned, in the empty nights.

A Charm of Goldfinches

Grey as a funeral day,
Sky like a wet sheet over the hedge,
Black stalks and piled leaves,
All colour gone, wind sharp as knives.

Then suddenly a shower
Chattering and squabbling,
A fall of gold from the tree,
A pirates' horde, a sultan's treasure,
Jewels in the gloom,
Goldfinches perform their winter alchemy
Reminding you that summer will soon return
In all its scarlet and gold.

Insect Noise

Sitting in a great bowl
Of hills, under sky's hot blue skull,
Not a tractor, bird, nor sheep;
It's midday, the time of huge silence.
Our lemonade warms in the sun.

The noise is tiny,
Just an insect buzz,
But up there somewhere in the blue
Crawls a real plane
Stuffed full of real people,
Who laugh, eat, play their machines.
They could drop a bomb, they wouldn't care;

We are just ants to them
And they just insect noise to us.
People die every day,
A long long way away;
They are small and distant, insect noise.
We adjust our hats in the sun,
And drink our lemonade before the ice melts.

St Ives

The fat man eats his chips one at a time,

A small boy complains that he's too hot.

The pretty tattooed waitress brings my coffee with a smile.

In a corner, a crisis is going on,

He imploring, she crying; I'll never find out.

Sun drenches the sea with light, and the sand shimmers.

Small impossible cottages tumble down to the shore,

Pastel-painted; Granny's Kot and Seagull View.

Nobody lives here now – the fishermen long gone.

Tourists gasp at the view and artists drink up the light.

It's beautiful here, just like they said.

But I suppose I'll never go back,

I'll never go back.

Evening Service

Winding up the hill,
Under a black starless sky,
They could be timeless, any time,
Carrying their faith before them,
To where they hope it dwells.

The window glows golden, golden,
Though inside the church will be cold and fusty,
Like the faith which most of them now have lost.

Does it matter? Still they
Climb the twisting hill,
As they have done for centuries,
And maybe will do for more;
The faint and fragile faith
Of that golden window
Still sustaining them
Through difficult days
And faithless times.

Jodi's Goats

Jodi keeps goats on the hill,

Three of them, all white, girls, I think.

They have their fenced-off square of grass, their goat world,

And there they live, days and nights, sunshine and rain.

The green world wraps around them,

Hills, hedges, the curving road, more hills, the great bowl of sky.

Sheep are in the fields, their distant cousins.

There are hundreds of them. They ignore each other

And keep on eating. Unlike their cousins, no-one will eat these
 goats.

Nothing interrupts their eating.

Sometimes they see us, lift up their heads.

They wonder what we're doing, why we don't stay still,

Why we haven't brought food,

Why we smell so strange, and make odd noises,

Why we don't eat the grass we walk on.

What kind of life is that?

They go on eating. Probably they don't give that much thought
 to us.

This autumn

Cloud takes up the mountain in a fist,

Squeezes it dry so that rain streams down the road

In a black shining river.

Scanty trees sway and drop pale leaves.

The wind shakes everything it can get hold of.

Mushrooms rot in the ground.

A spring frost killed all the blossom,

So we have no golden apples –

Something is killing all our rowan trees.

Dying hornets batter our window like little gold missiles.

Even the slugs are…well, sluggish.

The earth is melting and filling up with itself.

They say it's here to stay.

Winter Birthday

After rain all day a moon rides high in shining clouds,

A ginger cat sits fatly in a neighbour's window,

While late in December, we celebrate a birthday

With wine, good food and presents wrapped in gold.

Though each birthday makes us older, we are glad to have them
    still,

Though year by year the world does not improve,

Though now it is run by the mad, the bad and the profligate,

We can find space to celebrate

And drive through black and winding roads,

Through ragged trees and crowding hills

Through meteor showers scattering light,

To an inn where we'll be fed and welcomed.

With candlelight and crystal glasses,

Pretending all the time that the world is not like it is,

That love is stronger than death and that good wins out,

And all the other lies they tell for comfort,

And that if another birthday comes next year

The world will be that better place.

Only on a birthday can we believe this.

The Silence of Time

Now clocks no longer tick
Time eats up the hours
Silently as a snake,
Now bells no longer ring,
People die, and the hours close over them.

Nothing sounds when friends break up,
And couples part and weddings die.

Sometimes, it stops altogether
And a space grows where the minutes were.

When I left my house of twenty years
I closed the door on the echoing fanlit hall
And paused a long moment before
Stuffing keys through the letterbox
And walking into the sun of an empty road
Down stone steps that were no longer mine.

Only Child

The door shuts, I am inside my room; there are stories there,
and worlds.

Other children play outside, I can't, but I don't miss their games.

My parents are enclosed in their love; I make a third.

I go where they go, tea with old ladies, trips to castle ruins.

I don't mind – I am making memories…

But now those memories unshared grow dim and fade;

The woods, with their honour guard of elms, like all elms now,
long dead.

And the ruined house, burned down one night by a tramp.

Neighbours – the nice, the racist; the loud northerner who loved
her golf;

The woman who never washed her curtains – my grandmother
noticed such things;

The monkey puzzle tree around the corner (whoever grows
them now?)

The fireside bookshelf, where I curled up in a chair to read,

Devouring Molly Bloom at ten – my parents never knew that.

Those raucous tulips on the wall – they preferred real paintings,
even bad ones.

The old black radio, with its flashing dial, full of crackling worlds,

The Aga, which went out one day when I was left in charge.

Our grouchy black cat, the little dog which my grandmother would kick

When she thought we didn't see.

The apple tree in the garden, with its fat sour fruits, too sour to cook.

Green woodpeckers on the lawn; the heavy clay which my father cursed,

But diligently dug; the cupboard we called the *cwtsh*, the red front door.

My mother's swirling skirts, my own white ankle socks

And new Clarks sandals every summer, that X-ray machine such fun,

The phone crouching in the hall like a big black frog.

The silver street lamp outside my window,

And the rain running down the glass at night making rainbows…

No-one to see these things now. Does it even matter,

In a world where great things happen, why care for small ones?

But I'd like to share those fragile, lowly tales,

As sisters do, and brothers do, not I.

If you enjoyed this book...

Authors work hard to be noticed in the crowded world of
books, and often it's word-of-mouth that makes
all the difference.

Please consider rating and reviewing this book on your
favourite book review site.

Thank you for your support and help.

www.ingramcontent.com/pod-product-compliance
Lightning Source LLC
LaVergne TN
LVHW041307080426
835510LV00009B/889